EYEWITNESS TO WAR

Australia's Pacific Campaign 1941-1945

MICHAEL ANDREWS

DREAMWEAVER

ACKNOWLEDGEMENTS

The publisher thanks the Australian War Memorial and
the National Library of Australia for supplying the photographs
which appear in this book.

Published by Dreamweaver

GPO Box 1546, Sydney NSW 2001, Australia

ISBN 0 949193 00 3

Copyright © 1985 S and L Brodie

First published 1985, reprinted 1994

Printed in Australia by McPherson's Printing Group

MALAYA

Indecision reigned in Singapore as the Japanese began their inexorable march south. Commander-in-Chief Air Chief Marshal Sir Robert Brooke-Popham received advice that pointed to a Japanese seaborne convoy either making its way across the Gulf of Siam to Thailand or heading for the Japan–Vichy-ruled Indo-China colonies. He hesitated about ordering the army to invade southern Thailand until he knew just what the Japanese were doing. By the time he found out it was too late.

On 7 December 1941 the Japanese convoy, with support from a large group of fighters and bombers, arrived off the coasts of Malaya and Thailand. Their first landings were at Kota Bahru in northern Malaya and Singora and Patani in Thailand.

Kota Bahru was defended by the 3 Dogras Battalion of the Indian Army, backed up by three battalions of the 8 Brigade and supported by aircraft

RAAF Lockheed Hudson bombers in flight over Malaya in 1941.

from the Royal Australian Air Force 1 Squadron. The defenders succeeded in sinking a Japanese troopship, but the Japanese quickly established a hold on the Kota Bahru area. The war had begun in earnest.

In Thailand the Japanese landed shortly before dawn. Royal Air Force Blenheim bombers which attacked the invaders at Patani were repelled by Japanese fighters; Japanese aircraft also attacked the RAAF base at Sungei Patani, wiping out a large number of Buffalo fighters.

Back home, Australians woke on 8 December to hear the news of the Japanese attack at Pearl Harbor. Prime Minister Curtin was advised just before six o'clock that morning. He broadcast from every radio station across the nation, calling on the people of Australia to rally to the support of their country.

Curtin was a very worried man. His worst fears had been realised: Australia lay open to attack while 120 000 of her best fighting men were on the other side of the world.

Australians began to think in terms of an assault on their own country like that at Pearl Harbor. Ranged against the superior Japanese air force was a group of Buffalo fighters, CAC Wirraway trainer fighters, Lockheed Hudson bombers and a few PBY Catalina flying boats, not to mention trainer aircraft such as deHavilland Tiger Moths.

The manpower of the Australian Army stood at around 300 000. But 120 000 of them were in the 6, 7 and 9 Divisions in North Africa and the Middle East and the 8 Division in Malaya.

To convince Australians that Singapore was impregnable the British administration flew Australians to the colony in 1941 to see and report the situation on the island.

Life in Singapore was slightly unreal for Australians who went there to fight a war. The soldiers found a colony which did not really believe it would be attacked.

Lieutenant-General Percival, commander of all military forces in Malaya at the time of the fall of Singapore.

The remainder consisted of 30 000 AIF volunteers training in Australia and the Militia, which could not be deployed outside Australian territory. Within five days of the Japanese attacks a further 114 000 men were called up. Recruiting stations were rushed by young men wanting to enlist in the AIF, and women's military and civilian groups were also swamped with applications for membership.

On 9 December the two great battleships HMS *Repulse* and HMS *Prince of Wales* were sunk in a fierce battle to the east of Singapore. The two ships and their attendant fleet had been without proper air cover and the Japanese air force had slaughtered them.

By Christmas Day 1941 the Japanese forces were advancing down the Malayan peninsula, had landed in the oil-rich British colony of Sarawak, had taken Hong Kong and the American islands of Guam and Wake, and were engaged in fighting with General Douglas Macarthur's troops in the Philippines.

Curtin was desperate to have some indication of military support from the Americans. When he experienced great difficulty impressing President Roosevelt of the gravity of

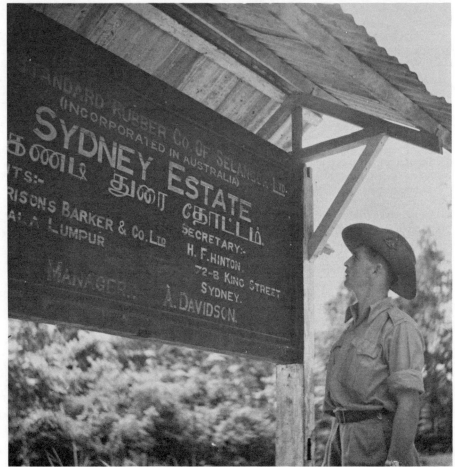

An Australian soldier finds a little bit of home in Malaya.

As the Japanese advanced through Malaya the roads became full of refugees fleeing south to escape the conquerers.

Australia's situation, he went public in a move designed to force the Americans into action. On 27 December, in the Melbourne *Herald* newspaper, Curtin wrote:

> The Australian Government, therefore, regards the Pacific struggle as primarily one in which the United States and Australia must have the fullest say in the direction of the democracies' fighting plan.
>
> Without any inhibitions of any kind, I make it quite clear that Australia looks to America, free of any pangs as to our traditional links or kinship with the United Kingdom.
>
> We know the problems that the United Kingdom faces. We known the constant threat of invasion. We know the dangers of dispersal of strength, but we know too that Australia can go and Britain can still hold on.

In early January 1942 there were moves to withdraw at least one Australian Division from the Middle East and Africa. Initially destined for Malaya, the troops were redirected to Sumatra in the Dutch East Indies. There now seemed little chance of the reinforce-

To ensure they did not fall into the hands of the Japanese, retreating Allied forces set fire to Malayan rubber stocks on plantation after plantation.

ments arriving in Malaya before it was overrun by the Japanese.

The defenders of Malaya had been forced into the southernmost third of the colony by the Japanese onslaught. Australian, Indian and British forces were being pushed back to Johore. Fierce fighting took place around the Muar River and Segamat in the west and around Mersing in the east.

An ambush was laid for the advancing Japanese along a road cutting south of the Gemencheh River by the Australian 2/30 Battalion. In the late afternoon more than 1000 Japanese troops riding bicycles started to cross the Gemencheh River bridge. The Australians destroyed the bridge and opened fire. Initially the assault was successful, but at a crucial moment the signal lines were cut and the Australian commander was unable to call up artillery bombardments to stop more Japanese fording the Gemencheh River.

Allied engineers in Malaya prepare to demolish a bridge to slow the Japanese advance.

Bicycles were the key to the Japanese invaders' great mobility.

Lack of ablution facilities often meant this was the only way of taking a bath in the war in Malaya.

not come to grips with the possibility of attack from the air and had made no provision for brown-outs or black-outs. Ablaze with lights, the island was first attacked by Japanese aircraft at night.

In early February the Japanese began artillery bombardments from across the Strait, causing considerable damage. On the evening of 8 February they launched an attack across the water to the west of the Johore Causeway and were engaged by the Australian 2/20 Battalion and a Chinese unit. Late in the afternoon of the next day Percival began planning a withdrawal to the city and harbour area in the south.

During the first days of February massive evacuations of civilians took place. Almost anything was pressed into service to move people out of the besieged city. Larger ships made for Batavia (Jakarta), smaller craft crossed the Straits of Malacca to Sumatra.

Sightseeing troops in 1941. For most Australian soldiers Malaya was a totally alien experience.

One of the prizes the Japanese found awaiting them at Singapore: the Royal Navy's massive floating dock, part of the superb dockyard facilities.

SINGAPORE

In late January 1942 Lieutenant-General Percival decided to withdraw the remaining Allied troops out of Johore to defend the island of Singapore. Once the troops were on the island a gap was blown in the Johore Causeway, the road link between the island and the mainland.

Singapore did not have enough food or water to maintain its own population, let alone the flood of refugees escaping the invasion. Without food supplies coming in from Malaya the Japanese could starve out the defenders.

In eight weeks the Japanese 25 Army, comprising around 35 000 men, had pushed a force of more than 60 000 Australians, Indians and British completely off the Malay peninsula. The scene was set for a massive and humiliating defeat.

Now only the Johore Strait separated the Japanese and Allied armies and for weeks the Japanese air force rained bombs on the town of Singapore. The authorities in Singapore had

The colonial splendour of Singapore's General Post Office. The front entrance was bricked up as a protection against bombings.

The Kalang flying boat base at Singapore. Anchored in the water are Empire flying boats of Qantas and Imperial Airways.

Looking across Johore Strait to the town of Johore Bahru. The Johore Causeway (in centre) was the only link between Singapore and the Malayan mainland. In the foreground a gun crew awaits the Japanese advance.

Smoke rises from the bombed city as Singapore experiences another Japanese onslaught.

Bomb damage to shop-houses in Singapore.

Wounded civilians are carried through Singapore streets in the wake of another Japanese bombing attack.

11

Black smoke billows from fires in oil storage tanks at the Royal Navy's base on the other side of Singapore island.

Percival ordered Australian Lieutenant-General Gordon Bennett to counter-attack on the western side of the island between Kranji and Jurong. He was thwarted by the swift-moving Japanese force nearing the outskirts of the city area on the 11th. Japanese aircraft began dropping leaflets calling on the defenders to surrender.

The only plan left now was to establish a perimeter defence around the city. It was obvious the island would fall within hours, but a perimeter would provide cover under which hospital and non-combatant military staff could be evacuated by sea. By the 14th the defenders realised that continued defence would result in wholesale slaughter. The situation was complicated by a critical shortage of water.

Percival received advice the next morning that Churchill was agreeable to a surrender. At this point Bennett, the senior Australian officer, escaped the doomed city by sailing across to

Parents entertain children waiting to be taken from Singapore by sea or air.

Japanese commanders accept the Allied surrender at Singapore.

Allied soldiers surrender to the Japanese invaders after the fall of Singapore.

Java from where he made his way to Australia. Made without Percival's authority, Bennett's departure from Singapore was one of the most controversial events of the war. He was vilified for not having stayed with his troops (some 16 000 men), but he firmly believed it was his duty to return home to report what had happened at Singapore.

In the afternoon of 15 February 1942 Percival made contact with the Japanese commander, General Yamashita. Just after eight o'clock that evening all fighting ceased and 130 000 Allied soldiers became prisoners of war.

Victorious Japanese troops march into the city of Singapore.

RAAF airmen (above) and soldiers (below) arrive back in Australia from Singapore. Not all Australian service personnel were captured when Singapore fell.

Lieutenant-General Gordon Bennett, who was severely criticised when he escaped from Singapore to return to Australia.

14

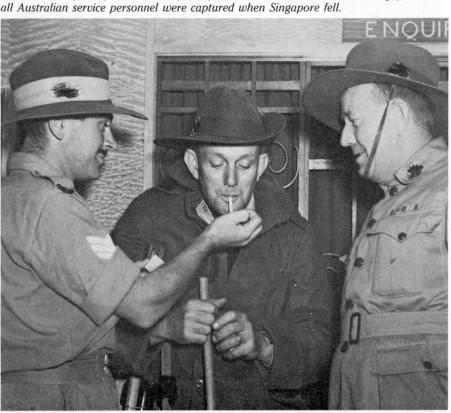

NEW BRITAIN AND NEW IRELAND

On 4 January 1942 the war came much closer to home when the Japanese began bombing raids on Rabaul, New Guinea, on the island of New Britain. This was the first occasion on which Japanese bombs had fallen on Australian territory. New Guinea was now the front line of defence for Australia.

Based at Rabaul was the 2/22 Battalion with just two coastal guns and two anti-aircraft guns. Supporting the troops were the tiny New Guinea Volunteer Rifles detachment and the 24 Squadron of the Royal Australian Air Force. The latter could boast eight CAC Wirraway trainers, which were being classed as fighters, and four Lockheed Hudson bombers.

The bombings of the two airfields at Rabaul from 4 January onwards were sporadic, but on 20 January a force of more than 100 aircraft flew in to attack the town. Ordered to retaliate, the 24 Squadron pilots of the eight Wirraways flew their aircraft into battle against the attackers in a show of great bravery and were shot to pieces.

In what was one of the most unfortunate events of the war, Japanese bombs hit an ammunition dump and the subsequent explosion shattered the valves of all the radio transmitters in Rabaul, cutting it off from the outside world.

Just after midnight that night the Japanese South Seas Force began its assault on New Britain. Landing craft reached the beaches of Keravia Bay and Simpson Harbour. By dawn the invaders were pushing the Australian defenders back from Rabaul. By the afternoon of 23 January it was all over. A large number of Australians had surrendered; others had fled south to evade capture.

At the same time, the Japanese landed on New Ireland just to the north of New Britain. The 1 Independent Company based at Kavieng was all but helpless and withdrew from the town after destroying any supplies it could not carry.

Soldiers of the New Guinea Volunteer Rifles march through Rabaul. (National Library of Australia photo)

AMBON AND TIMOR

During December 1941 the Australian 2/21 Battalion had arrived at Ambon in the Dutch East Indies. A small island on the south-western tip of the larger island of Seram, Ambon was part of the Molucca group just west of Dutch New Guinea. The Australian government had agreed to Australian troops being sent to reinforce the Dutch garrisons at Ambon and Timor in the event of war breaking out with Japan.

Ambon was attacked by Japanese aircraft on 6 January as Japanese land forces made their way south through the poorly defended Celebes and Molucca islands. After a prolonged campaign of attack by carrier-based aircraft, on 31 January the Japanese moved to an amphibious assault on Ambon at Hitu-Lama on the northern coast. From there they quickly established themselves on land and forged across to the island's main defences on the Laitimor Peninsula. They were joined by forces which subsequently had landed in Baguala Bay. The numerically superior Japanese force pushed the resisting Australians and Dutch into the town of Eri, where they surrendered.

Australian troops were stationed in the western half of Timor, which belonged to the Dutch. The east was a colony of neutral Portugal. During December West Timor was reinforced by the 2/40 Battalion and 2/2 Independent Company, bringing the defence force to almost 2000 including a group of around 500 indigenous soldiers with Dutch commanders. To strengthen the defences part of the force was despatched to Dili, capital of Portugese Timor.

The Japanese began bombing Timor on 26 January. A Qantas Empire flying boat en route to Singapore on 30 January was attacked by seven Japanese fighters within sight of Koepang, Dutch Timor. Its pilot dropped the aircraft to water level in an attempt to evade the attackers, but the damage was too great and he was forced to ditch it in the water close to the coastline.

On 19 February the Japanese landed a force near Dili and attacked the 2 Independent Company guarding the airfield. The attackers encountered fierce defence and suffered heavy casualties. Next day the Company rendered the airfield unusable and withdrew just as the Japanese landed near Koepang. The fighting on Timor was some of the fiercest seen so far in the war. On 23 February the Japanese demanded the Australians' surrender. Realising their position was hopeless some Australians did so, but others moved into the rugged hinterland to begin a protracted guerrilla war.

RETURN FROM AFRICA

The Singapore debacle raised questions vital to the defence of Australia. When the situation in Malaya deteriorated General Wavell decided to land the Australians coming back from Africa and the Middle East at Sumatra (6 Division) and Java (7 Division). It was assumed that, after Singapore, Sumatra and Java would be next as the Japanese were moving through Borneo and the Celebes islands. Curtin's military advisers argued that once Singapore fell the Japanese army would mount an all-out assault on the Dutch East Indies.

While the dispute continued the 2/3 Machine-Gun Battalion and the 2/2 Pioneer Battalion of the Australian Imperial Force arrived at Batavia from Africa and were assigned to guard vital airfields. Australia's Lieutenant-General John Lavarack argued that the troops should not be used in Java, which Australia regarded as a lost cause. Wavell, not wanting to abandon the Dutch colonialists, insisted the Australians remain at Batavia.

One day before the surrender at Singapore the United States administration decided to make Australia its main base for the war against Japan. Almost immediately the American 41 Division was ordered to Australia. This new development led the Australian Chiefs of Staff to argue vigorously for the entire 6 and 7 Divisions to return to Australia rather than be sent to the Dutch East Indies. The troops were still at sea and could easily be diverted. A plan hatched by the British to send the Australians to Burma was opposed by Curtin, who considered Burma a lost cause because it lacked air power.

Churchill ordered the troop convoy to make for Burma; Curtin countered with a request that the 100 000 troops be brought home. Outraged, Churchill insisted the Australians go wherever the British military wanted. He appealed to Roosevelt for assistance in swaying Curtin and between them they exerted great pressure on the Australian Prime Minister. Roosevelt assured Curtin that he would send American troops to Australia if the Australians went to Burma.

At the same time as he made an urgent plea to Curtin to change his mind, Churchill ordered the troopships to head for Rangoon. Curtin stood his ground, forcing an angry Churchill to relent. The ships turned for home.

passed over Bathurst Island and Catholic missionaries based there radioed Darwin. Believing the missionaries to be mistaken, the RAAF refused to act on the advice. As the formation began its run over the city the population went out to watch, thinking the planes were American.

Within minutes a torrent of high explosives began dropping from the sky. Japanese aircraft roared in over the town, strafing the harbour and the airfield. After the first attack, which had done most of its damage in the town and the harbour, a second wave swept in just before midday and concentrated on the airfield.

Virtually unopposed, the attackers left Darwin almost completely destroyed. The airfield was a shambles with a large number of RAAF and USAAF aircraft wrecked. In the harbour Australian troopships had been sunk along with the American destroyer USS *Peary* and a number of cargo vessels. The death toll stood at 243 — more than half of whom had been on the ships in the harbour — with 350 wounded.

Psychologically unprepared for attack, the population understandably panicked. The civilians took to the road in cars, trucks, motor cycles or on foot.

But the level of panic among servicemen was deplorable. During the

DARWIN

O n 19 February 1942 war came to Australia for the first time since white settlement.

From a point off the coast of Timor a fleet of around 200 Japanese aircraft was despatched to attack Darwin. Early in the morning the aircraft

Building huts for troops near Darwin.

A convoy of young troops arrives to bolster Darwin's defences.

Smoke from burning ships, buildings and oil tanks rises over Darwin in the wake of the Japanese air raid.

bombing numerous servicemen deserted their posts and took to the road with the civilians. In the town, once the fires had been stopped and the dead and injured attended to, a mood of relief was apparent. Drunken Provost Corps troops took advantage of the swift desertion of the town by looting shops left behind by civilian proprietors.

Damage done by Japanese bombs to the Bank of New South Wales branch in Darwin.

The lightweight houses of Darwin were no match for the Japanese bombing attacks.

Defence against invasion — barbed wire on a Darwin beach.

Wrecked RAAF aircraft at Darwin air base.

Shops with shattered windows in a Darwin street.

Inspecting damage to a house in Darwin.

An air raid shelter in Hyde Park, Sydney, locked up to prevent vandalism and thereby becoming almost useless.

Army barracks wrecked in the Japanese bombing attack on Darwin.

Australian and American soldiers march along Elizabeth Street, Sydney.

JAVA

Fortunately for Australia the air raid on Darwin was not a prelude to invasion. It was intended merely to neutralise the port of Darwin to allow the Japanese 16 Army to invade Java.

Australian units involved in the defence of Java included the 2/3 Machine-Gun Battalion, 2/2 Pioneer Battalion, 2/2 Field Company, 2/2 Casualty Clearing Station and 105 General Transport Company. The units were poorly equipped: the Machine-Gun Battalion had no machine-guns whatsoever. They were on ships bringing the forces from the Middle East. On the water were two RAN cruisers — HMAS *Perth* and HMAS *Hobart* — part of a fleet comprising Dutch, American, British and Australian ships.

On 25 February reconnaissance aircraft reported two Japanese invasion fleets making for Java — one for the east, the other for the west. A navy force including *Perth* sailed out against the eastern fleet, while *Hobart* took part in a move against the western. Two days later the eastern fleet engaged the enemy in a ferocious battle in which two cruisers and four destroyers of the Allied navy were sunk. In the west the fleet was unable to find the Japanese, apparently because Japanese reconnaissance had mistaken the Allied cruisers for battleships and their destroyers for cruisers, causing the enemy to avoid a confrontation.

In company with USS *Houston*, on 1 March HMAS *Perth* went looking for the Japanese and found them by chance. In the subsequent fierce battle the two cruisers destroyed a Japanese troop transport; however both were sunk by the superior Japanese force.

The Japanese were able to land troops on Java in three places during the night of 28 February. Heavy casualties were inflicted on the defenders and by 6 March Java was lost. On 12 March Lieutenant-Colonel Blackburn surrendered to the Japanese at Bandung.

The post-Darwin bombing period saw many large city buildings, such as this Commonwealth Bank in Melbourne, bricked up to minimise bomb damage.

NEW GUINEA

Early in March 1942 the Japanese moved to take the New Guinea mainland. Opposed by only a small local force of New Guinea Volunteer Rifles, they landed at Lae and Salamaua. This gave

them a good base from which to sever supply lines between the USA and Australia. The NGVR troops retreated inland to the gold-mining centre of Wau in the highlands, using their intimate knowledge of the region to harry the Japanese regularly.

Port Moresby, most likely the next Japanese target, was assigned the 53 Battalion. It joined the 49 Battalion there in January 1942. Both battalions were poorly trained and ill-equipped for the rigours of war in Papua–New Guinea. Their situation was not helped by the almost constant attacks of Japanese fighters and bombers. In late March the air defences were reinforced by 75 Squadron of the RAAF. Although losses were heavy, the Kittyhawk fighters gave the enemy their first real resistance.

Soldiers of the Light Horse in New Guinea.

Nurses arriving at Port Moresby in 1942.

25

Australian and Dutch troops in New Guinea.

An RAAF Bristol Beaufort bomber in action.

Bomb loads for RAAF Beauforts in New Guinea.

Preparing belts of cartridges for machine guns.

Firing an anti-aircraft gun located at Port Moresby.

Engineering units construct an airstrip in New Guinea.

An RAAF Vengeance dive-bomber prepares for take-off.

Natives rolling the surface of an RAAF airstrip in New Guinea.

Loading copies of the Guinea Gold *newspaper aboard a C47 transport aircraft for distribution to troops.*

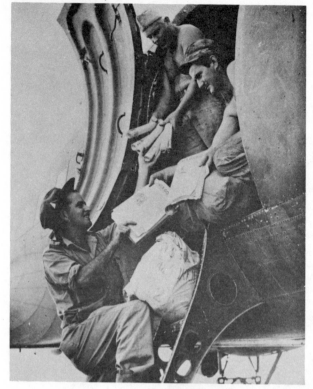

Mail from home.

Troops pinned down on a beach by Japanese gunfire.

Preparing an edition of Guinea Gold, *a newspaper for troops in New Guinea.*

Handing out magazines to soldiers eager for news from home.

31

Bakers preparing bread for troops in New Guinea.

An Australian soldier with a captured Samurai sword.

Censoring mail sent by troops to families and friends back home.

Australian soldiers supervise New Guinea native bearers taking supplies to the battlefront.

33

Draining a New Guinea swamp in an endeavour to cut down the incidence of malaria among Australian troops.

Carrying wounded soldiers on a Jeep.

One of the many Salvation Army posts which provided soldiers with some comforts during the New Guinea campaigns.

Time for relaxation and a meal.

Prime Minister John Curtin and General Douglas Macarthur at Parliament House, Canberra.

Prime Minister John Curtin with General Douglas Macarthur.

MACARTHUR

By mid-March 1942 the Japanese had taken Hong Kong, French Indo-China, Burma, Thailand, Malaya, the Dutch East Indies, New Guinea, Guam and Wake Islands, and much of the Philippines. The only continuing resistance came from the Americans on the Philippine island of Luzon, Australians on Timor, and the British Indian forces retreating in Borneo. For the Japanese the two great targets ahead were Australia and India.

Vast quantities of American troops and equipment were arriving in Australia. The Australian 6 and 7 Divisions had arrived home and were being prepared for the war in Papua–New Guinea.

During the last bitter days of fighting in the Philippines the US commander, General Douglas Macarthur, was ordered to Australia. On 19 March Macarthur arrived in Darwin and made his way to Melbourne. For a week he waited in a Melbourne hotel while arrangements between Australia and the USA were thrashed out. Finally he became Commander-in-Chief of Allied forces in the South-West Pacific. Three commanding officers were appointed: General Thomas Blamey (Australia) as Commander of the Allied Land Forces, Lieutenant-General George Brett (USA) as Commander of the Allied Air Forces, and Vice-Admiral Herbert Leary (USA) as Commander of the Allied Navies. The work of putting up a creditable defence against the seemingly invincible Japanese forces had begun.

FIGHTING BACK

Of the few places where the Japanese invasion was still being resisted in early 1942, one was Timor and another was the Wau–Salamaua–Lae area in New Guinea.

On Timor the Australian 2/2 Independent Company maintained a guerrilla war against the Japanese, thwarting strong attempts to flush them out. The guerrillas were kept supplied by airdrops from the RAAF base at Darwin.

The New Guinea Volunteer Rifles' incursions against the Japanese at Lae and Salamaua proved so successful they were reinforced by the 2/5 Independent Company. Between them the NGVR and the Independents were able to keep more Japanese troops tied up in the region than should have been necessary.

CORAL SEA

During April 1942 the Japanese prepared to attack the Papuan town of Port Moresby. Success in this venture would provide them with a base from which air raids could be made on the Australian mainland. In the first week of May Japanese troopships, accompanied by a large number of fighting ships, set out from New Guinea.

But, unknown to the Japanese, the Americans had broken their signal codes. The Allies decided to engage the Japanese as they rounded the tip of Papua. When the Japanese realised a fleet (which included the cruisers HMAS *Australia* and HMAS *Hobart*) was waiting to engage them, the troop transports were sent back. Aircraft from USS *Lexington* and USS *Yorktown* attacked and sank the small Japanese carrier *Shoho* on 7 May. The following day aircraft from *Lexington* and *Yorktown* clashed with those from *Zuikaku* and *Shokaku*. At day's end both *Yorktown* and *Shokaku* were damaged, but still operational.

The 'Battle of the Coral Sea' was an enormous psychological victory for the Allies. Although there was no decisive victory in terms of ships sunk or aircraft destroyed, for the first time the Japanese had turned back.

MIDGET SUBMARINES

For the people of Sydney May 1942 ended spectacularly. On Sunday 31 May five Japanese submarines, including three midget submarine mother ships, arrived off Sydney in the Tasman Sea. Three midget submarines were sent to raid Sydney Harbour, which was crammed with Allied naval and merchant shipping. Two midgets made it past the anti-submarine boom across the entrance to the harbour; the third became hopelessly entangled in the net. The two made their way to Garden Island Naval Base.

A torpedo fired at the American cruiser USS *Chicago* missed its target. Instead it hit HMAS *Kuttabul*, a former Sydney ferry converted to a Navy stores ship. The ferry sank almost immediately, drowning nineteen naval ratings asleep on board.

Searchlights and flares lit the water and ships dropped depth charges. At sunrise it was found one of the submarines had been hit and the other had disappeared. The crew of the midget caught in the anti-submarine net had opted for suicide by detonating explosives carried on board. Among residents of the eastern suburbs the attack brought on a wave of hysteria. Those who could afford it closed up their homes and headed west to the Blue Mountains.

Early on 8 June a Japanese submarine surfaced off Sydney and fired a number of rounds, causing a small amount of damage to houses in Bellevue Hill, Woollahra and Rose Bay. Another submarine made a similar attack on Newcastle.

The result of a Japanese submarine shelling Sydney's eastern suburbs.

One of the midget submarines which raided Sydney and sank the converted ferry HMAS Kuttabul.

KOKODA TRACK

It was expected that the Japanese would now try to take Port Moresby by land. Most likely such an attack force would approach along a foot track which meandered over the Owen Stanley Ranges from the towns of Gona and Buna on the northern coast, through the Kokoda Pass, to Port Moresby. The Papuan Infantry Battalion was despatched to Buna to secure the area.

Unfortunately the PIB force was not quick enough. On 22 July 1942 the Japanese landed in strength at Gona. Australian defences in the region were very thin and the 300 men of the PIB were spread out between Buna and Kokoda awaiting reinforcement by the 39 Battalion. By 29 July the Australian and Papuan troops had been pushed back into the highlands and driven south of Kokoda. They mounted a counter-attack and retook Kokoda on 8 August, but the Japanese retaliated.

Once more the Australians and Papuans were forced south, and by 14 August the defenders were running low on food and water.

At Port Moresby the garrison was reinforced with units of the 7 Division. The 39 Battalion, fighting a losing battle on the Kokoda Track, was to be augmented by the 53 Battalion. Embattled forces along the track were close to starvation. Seldom were more than a couple of aircraft available for supply drops, although newly arriving troops brought hundreds of native bearers who formed a supply line between Port Moresby and the front. The renewed effort along the Kokoda Track began to falter. In late August the 39 Battalion was withdrawn, and on the 26th the Japanese again began to advance,

Soldiers receive goods from the Australian Comforts Fund (ACF).

nine Brigades. In late September a dispute developed between Blamey and the New Guinea force commander, Lieutenant-General Sydney Rowell, over Blamey's habit of issuing orders direct to Rowell's subordinates rather than through the correct channels. Blamey agreed to a more formalised chain of command then took direct control of the New Guinea campaign, relieving Rowell of his command.

During the first week of October the Japanese withdrew from their forward lines at Ioribaiwa. The 25 Brigade and 3 Battalion pursued them for a week, but their advance was hampered by the continuing lack of supplies. Airdropping techniques in the dense jungles were still amateurish and considerable quantities of *materiel* and rations were lost.

making considerable headway in the face of stiff opposition.

Conditions on the Kokoda Track were appalling. Troops battled on in torrential rain, in slime and mud, unable to prepare hot meals. Morale deteriorated rapidly among the young, inexperienced soldiers. It was difficult to move out the wounded in the wet and boggy conditions. Fresh troops were gradually brought up to relieve the exhausted and starving defenders. But by early September the Japanese were also beginning to falter.

Macarthur was distinctly edgy about the lack of results in the region and in mid-September expressed his concern to the Australian government. He claimed he had lost faith in the abilities of Australian troops to defend Papua — even though he had not been there himself to witness the abysmal conditions. Blamey toured the area and reported favourably on the efforts of the Australians, but this was not sufficient for Macarthur.

After Blamey's visit the Port Moresby garrison reached a strength of

A YMCA station providing some home comforts for troops during the Kokoda campaign.

The famous stretcher bearers who brought wounded soldiers out of the jungle.

When the Australians pushed to retake the village of Kokoda they met with strong resistance at Templeton's Crossing. Between 12 and 15 October the 3 Battalion, 2/33 Battalion and 2/25 Battalion engaged the enemy. By the 15th the enemy was withdrawing.

On 28 October the 2/1 and 2/3 Battalions engaged in a ferocious battle with the enemy at Eora Creek. It was a major success. On 2 November the 25 Brigade entered Kokoda village, abandoned by the retreating Japanese. The Australians now had control of an airfield into which supplies could be flown.

The 25 Brigade, 16 Brigade and 2/1 Battalion had Japanese troops trapped at Gorari with only broken units fleeing north by 9 November, and on 13 November 1942 the Australians reached the Kumusi River. The battle for the Kokoda Track was over.

Unloading bags containing Christmas parcels for troops in 1942.

Blamey speaks to a wounded soldier during a hospital visit.

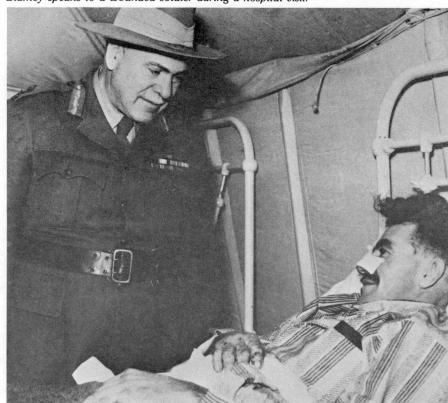

MILNE BAY

The Allies decided to construct an airstrip at Milne Bay on the far south-eastern tip of Papua. A small force of Australian soldiers sent into the area on 22 June 1942 was joined seven days later by American engineers who began rapid construction of the new base.

During the first week of July the Australian 7 Brigade arrived at Milne Bay, followed later by the 75 and 76 Squadrons of the RAAF with Kittyhawk fighters. On 12 August the 18 Brigade and artillery of the 2/5 Field Regiment also joined them.

Landing-craft delivered a Japanese assault force to Ahioma on the northern shore of Milne Bay, east of the Australian positions, on the night of 25 August. Fighting began early the next morning between the Australians and the westward-moving Japanese. RAAF Kittyhawk fighters and Hudson bombers attacked the Japanese landing-craft and supply depots. Throughout the following night and morning the Japanese made considerable advances with the aid of tanks, forcing the Australians to withdraw across the Gama River. In the skies over Milne Bay the Kittyhawks engaged Japanese dive-bombers and Zero fighters in the skies.

Raising the Australian flag at Kokoda. In the foreground is a Japanese memorial post.

43

The rugged mountains which fringe Milne Bay — some of the slopes drop straight to the edge of the water.

The wrecked hulk of the Japanese cargo ship Anshun *lies in shallow water in Milne Bay.*

Troops preparing for the trip ashore in landing-craft at Milne Bay.

Fierce battles ensued as the Japanese attempted to gain control of the airfield. The RAAF aircraft were flown out to Port Moresby. Gradually the Australians and a small contingent of Americans turned the tide, and on 4 September the Japanese commanders ordered an evacuation. For the first time Allied ground forces had inflicted a significant defeat on the Japanese army. To add to the triumph the victory was won by Militia units with only six-to-nine months' training behind them.

Australia celebrated the victory with enthusiasm: the Japanese were not invincible after all. The bravery at Milne Bay was highlighted by the posthumous awarding of the Victoria Cross to Corporal J A French of the 2/9 Battalion. In the last hours of the battle on 4 September 1942 French had advanced alone to destroy three Japanese machine-gun posts, dying as he took the third.

The beach at Milne Bay where landing-craft brought supplies ashore for the Australian units.

Soldiers trudge through the mud and slime of Milne Bay.

A soldier with the Australian designed and manufactured Owen gun in the jungle at Sanananda.

GONA

The next major objective set by Allied command was to take the villages of Gona, Buna and Sanananda on the northern coast of Papua.

Australian and American units were pushing the Japanese back towards Gona. On 19 November 1942 the 25 Brigade formed a semicircle around Gona, but the Japanese were determined to resist until the last. After several days of fighting the Australians were withdrawn, mostly because they were too far ahead of their supply lines and malaria was taking a heavy toll among the troops.

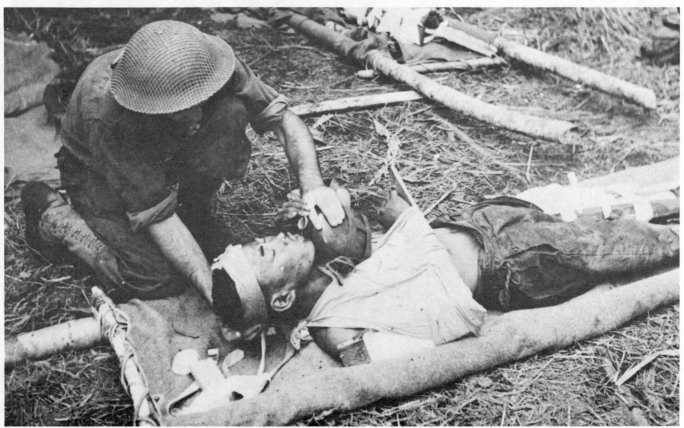

Wounded Japanese prisoners are given medical attention during the Gona campaign.

Burying dead Japanese at Gona.

Reinforced by the 2/31 and 2/33 Battalions, another attack was launched on Gona on 22 November. They were joined the following day by the 2/25 Battalion. Despite a number of assaults on enemy positions, however, the Australians were able to gain little ground and suffered heavy casualties. Allied commanders ordered the 21 Brigade airlifted into the battle zone (movement of troops by aircraft had become relatively common by this time).

Preparing to carry a wounded soldier out of the Gona battle area. *Bodies of Japanese soldiers killed during*

On 28 November Allied aircraft from Port Moresby laid down a heavy bombardment on Gona. Still the Japanese held their positions, inflicting heavy losses on the Australians. Diseases such as dysentery and malaria were continuing to reduce the Australian troop stength, but the Japanese were not immune either.

The relatively fresh troops of the 21 Brigade were thrown into the battle on 8 December. In a blistering assault half the Japanese positions fell to the Australians, ending organised resistance. By late the following day the 21 Brigade was in command of Gona.

the Gona battles.

A wounded soldier takes some welcome refreshment during the battle for Gona.

Graves of Australian soldiers killed at Gona.

As more and more American troops arrived Macarthur was eager for them to take part in the campaigns hitherto fought mostly by Australians. The Commander-in-Chief was desperate to obtain some of the 'glory' for his own country's forces. Large numbers of ill-prepared American servicemen were thrust into battles for which they had no training.

Buna proved a different story from Gona. In this village, east of Gona, the Japanese had the advantage of being up against troops who were not as well trained. The Americans found the going slow, prompting Macarthur to order an assessment of the situation. Lieutenant-General Robert Eichelberger found a demoralised force suffering from disease, heat exhaustion and poor lines of supply. They had not been prepared for the horrendous conditions encountered in the wet and humid

BUNA

In order to improve the chances of the forces on the Kokoda Track, the American 32 Division was sent to attack Buna, on the northern coast, from the southeast. Units of the 2/10 Battalion, 2/6 Independent Company and the American 128 Regiment were flown into Wanigela. From there troops were to secure the airfield at Pongani so that the force could be flown closer to Buna. The American 126 Battalion had also set out from the south to cross the ranges by the Juare Track, east of the Kokoda route.

Australian soldiers in action at Buna.

Australian troops with tank support fight their way through a palm tree plantation near Buna.

lowlands. On 5 December Blamey ordered in the Australian 2/9 Battalion and 2/6 Armoured Regiment, equipped with American M3 light tanks, as reinforcements. Eichelberger's report to Macarthur resulted in considerably increased air supplies.

The 2/9 Battalion moved in to replace the beleagured Americans, some of whom were starving and dressed in little more than rags. With the M3 tanks the Australians made significant progress, reaching Cape Endaiadere near the airfield. Two days later the troops battled toward Buna, coming under heavy mortar bombardment at Simeni Creek.

Units of the American 126 Regiment which had fought its way over the Juare Track joined the Australians on 24 December. Closer to Buna the Allied troops suffered a major setback when anti-aircraft guns in the village

Troops cross a fast-flowing river near Buna.

Soldiers prepare to move forward after a tank has cleared the way for them. Units with tank support were able to advance much faster than those without.

were turned on their tanks. The enemy scored direct hits on the M3s, the Australians' trump card.

On 31 December the 2/12 Battalion arrived to replace the 2/9th, which had spearheaded the advance against Buna. These fresh Australian troops, backed up by units of the American 128 Regiment, launched an assault on the area around Giropa Point on New Year's Day and broke the Japanese defence. Fighting all but ended on 3 January, with Japanese resistance almost nil.

Advancing through the jungle around Buna.

SANANANDA

Having captured Gona, the forces there were ordered to move on Sanananda which lay between Gona and Buna. Between 7 and 14 December 1942 the Australian–American contingent was considerably reinforced by the 7 Cavalry Regiment (operating as an infantry unit rather than in its conventional role of a mechanised force), 36 Battalion, 14 Brigade, 30 Brigade and the American 126 Regiment.

The reconstituted force began to move on Sanananda on 14 December. In its first engagement at Huggins

A Japanese truck riddled with bullet holes at Giropa Point.

Road-Block, three kilometres from the coast, the 7 Cavalry Regiment suffered severe casualties. Surrounded by the Japanese, the unit was cut off from the main Australian force. Several days passed before the besieged Cavalrymen could be relieved.

Fighting moved slowly until mid-January when more troops from Buna were brought into the action. The Japanese were pushed towards the coast and encircled in the village of Sanananda. Tanks were brought into play, but the enemy positions were well defended. On 13 January the enemy began a gradual withdrawal by sea.

They continued fighting until 22 January when all but sporadic Japanese resistance had ended. Although Allied forces still came under occasional attack from small bands of Japanese soldiers, the Buna–Sanananda–Gona region was secure.

TIMOR

On the island of Timor battles between Japanese forces and Australian units still raged. The 2/2 and 2/4 Independent Companies remained on the island, hiding in the mountainous country with the assistance of the native population and harassing the enemy. They were supplied by air-drops and by sea, but after the Australian destroyer HMAS *Voyager* ran aground on a supply mission the Japanese became more vigilant around the coast. By December 1942 the Independent Companies, who had fought well against the Japanese for a year, were suffering from disease and exhaustion.

The Allied commanders decided to withdraw the units. A Dutch destroyer *Tjerk Hiddes* made several forays into enemy waters to collect most of the troops between 10 and 19 December; the remainder were collected by HMAS *Arunta* on 11 January.

The atrocious muddy conditions at Sanananda. Mud, rain and disease were facts of life for Australians fighting in New Guinea.

54

WAU

In the highlands, around the gold-mining towns of Wau and Bulolo, Australian troops known as 'Kanga Force' had held off the Japanese who were well entrenched on the coast at Salamaua and as far inland as Mubo. Occasionally the Australians made raids into enemy territory because the Japanese were reluctant to move inland through the incredibly rough jungle country.

Allied command considered the defenders at Wau were ideally placed for an assault on Japanese positions at Lae and Madang. Kanga Force's main asset was Wau airstrip, and during October 1942 the force was strengthened by the arrival of the 2/7 Independent Company. On 11 January 1943 the reinforced units of Kanga Force moved quietly through the jungle to surround the Japanese at Mubo. But the Australians made little ground and ultimately were driven back by the enemy.

Kanga Force was withdrawn and replaced by the 17 Brigade. At much the same time the Japanese, fearing a troop buildup at Wau, took the offensive. On 28 January, after an arduous climb up a little-trafficked pathway to the east which became known as the 'Jap Track', the enemy launched an attack on Wandumi, east of Wau. The Australians at Wandumi were overrun.

During the night the enemy advanced to within four kilometres of Wau, engaging in heavy combat with the Australian defenders. Reinforcements ordered in from Port Moresby were delayed when heavy cloud made flying impossible. It was a frantic night and the commanders at Wau lost contact with a number of their units battling in the jungle.

Then the cloud lifted. Transport aircraft made sixty landings at Wau that day, bringing in more than 800 soldiers of the 2/5 and 2/7 Battalions. On 1 February the Australians, assisted by field artillery, launched a counter-attack and inflicted severe losses on the Japanese. Wau airfield, where transport aircraft were unloading, was subjected to attack by Japanese bombers and fighters. The enemy was fought off by aircraft of the RAAF.

By 9 February the Japanese were back where they had started, in the village of Mubo. Further reinforcement of the Wau contingent by units of the 4 and 15 Brigades on 13 February set the stage for an advance on Mubo.

MUBO

By April 1943 the Australians had reached Mubo and engaged the Japanese defenders. Assaults on Green Hill and The Pimple, two mountains just east of Mubo, were repulsed by the Japanese. On 4 May the 2/3 Independent Company attacked Japanese entrenched at Bobdubi Ridge, dislodging the defenders and taking the high ground. The Japanese threw themselves into numerous offences against the Australian position but failed to regain it. Another attack launched by the Australians on The Pimple was again defeated.

To relieve the hard-pressed 2/7th, the 2/6 Battalion was brought in. This led to a plan to take Nassau Bay, south-east of Mubo, an ideal jumping-off place for an amphibious assault on Lae. American landing-craft made the journey under cover of darkness and Allied forces attacked Japanese positions around Nassau Bay between 20 and 23 June. As usual the defenders held their positions until the very last moment. Only after suffering considerable casualties did the Australians take the bay, greatly aided by support from RAAF Beaufighter aircraft which strafed the enemy positions.

On the night of 29 June and during the following morning a fleet of thirty-two landing craft arrived at Nassau Bay. Total confusion reigned as numerous craft missed the landing area. By 6 July some 1500 troops had been landed at Nassau Bay along with supplies and equipment.

The intention was that the Allied units would move inland to the village of Napier. From there the Americans would make an assault on Bitoi Ridge while the Australians once more attempted to take Green Hill and the rest of The Pimple.

Further north the Australian 58/59 Battalion was fighting the Japanese at Bobdubi Ridge. Its attack on the village of Old Vickers on 9 July was unsuccessful. Meanwhile, to the south, the 2/3 Independent Company had taken Wells Junction. On the coast a unit of the Papuan Infantry was leading the American 162 Regiment northwards, with Tambu Bay as their objective.

Emphasis now returned to the Mubo region as the Australian–American force moved in. On 7 July RAAF Mitchell bombers attacked the village and the Observation Hill area before the 2/6 Battalion went in. By evening only isolated pockets of resistance remained. The advance continued: The Pimple fell to the Australians on 12 July, Mubo airfield and Green Hill the next day.

Between 16 and 19 July the 2/5 Battalion was engaged in a bitter fight for control of Mount Tambu. The Australians won much of the mountain on 16 July, but a small pocket of fiercely resisting Japanese remained. On 18 July a bloody battle took place in which a large number of Japanese were killed.

Considerable difficulty was still being experienced by the Australians around Bobdubi Ridge. Knowing this would be their last chance to hold the land route between Salamaua and Lae, the Japanese fought with grim determination. The 2/3 Independent Company took Ambush Knoll on 15 July, but the enemy counter-attacked. Also pushing towards Bobdubi, the 58/59 Battalion had not been as successful as the Independents.

On 28 July 1943 units of the 58/59 Battalion launched a concerted attack on Bobdubi Ridge, taking it in a fierce battle.

Australian soldiers join up with American units at Nassau Bay near Mubo.

SALAMAUA

The final phase of the battle for Salamaua now began. Australian, American and Papuan units had taken Komiatum and Davidson Ridge and cleared the last of the enemy from around Mount Tambu. The 15 Brigade was closing in on Salamaua against heavy Japanese opposition. By late August 1943 the enemy was all but isolated around the coastal village. A final attack was delayed until the major assault on Lae commenced.

Once the landings had taken place near Lae, Allied forces were able to move on the Japanese garrison with the knowledge that no reinforcements would be coming from Lae.

LAE

Bottling up the Japanese forces in the Salamaua region allowed the Allies to begin final planning for an attack on the heavily fortified town of Lae, just to the north. After Lae their objective would be the Japanese concentrations in the Ramu and Markham River Valleys.

The plan was to land a force on beaches east of Lae. On the first two days of September 1943 the 20 and 26 Brigades were carried in landing vessels from Milne Bay along the coast

of Papua to Buna. Then on 4 September the fleet, numbering over 150 craft, pushed on from Buna to its destination. A fleet of destroyers laid down a heavy barrage on the region around the beach before the troops of the 2/13, 2/15 and 2/17 Battalions made the journey to shore.

Landings took place at 'Yellow Beach' and 'Red Beach'. Initially there was no opposition, but within thirty minutes Japanese aircraft were attacking the landing-craft heading for the shore. The enemy aircraft were repelled by a group of USAAF fighters. An American construction unit with earth-moving equipment was landed to aid the advance of the invasion party. By mid-afternoon almost 8000 troops and supplies had been landed.

The first troops ashore moved quickly inland, advancing to the Buso River with little opposition, while the 2/2 Pioneer Battalion pushed overland to the village of Kirklands. Support also came from the 2/24 Battalion located in the Markham River Valley. The bitterest fighting on that day was at Markham Point, where Australian units assaulted a strongly defended Japanese position only to be repulsed after a long and difficult battle.

Troops of the 2/23 Battalion engaged Japanese forces east of Lae. Heavy rain all but halted the fighting and almost immediately flooded the Basu River. The only way to cross was for engineering units to construct a bridge. Under enemy fire soldiers battled their way across the raging water to establish a bridgehead on the opposite bank. Thirteen drowned in the attempt.

As the units of the 7 Division closed in on Lae Japanese opposition became more intense. A ferocious battle fought by the 2/31 and 2/33 Battalions at Edwards Plantation cleared the way for a move on Lae. This was premature, however, as artillery gunners and the air force were unaware of their presence and the units retreated with casualties inflicted by their own side. The short time spent in Lae had revealed almost a complete ruin — the result of Allied bombardment — but few Japanese defenders.

Coming ashore from landing-craft at Saidor.

HUON PENINSULA

Having forced the enemy out of the Lae area, the Allies decided to remove them altogether from the Huon Peninsula, north and east of Lae. This manoeuvre was vital to the success of the planned assault on the Japanese garrison on New Britain. Around Finschhafen, on the Peninsula, the Japanese had a large concentration of ground forces as well as a naval base and a busy airfield.

On 22 September 1944, preceded by a savage bombardment from Allied

Australian troops meet up with American soldiers in the Huon Peninsula campaign.

Australian troops crossing the Song River on the Huon Peninsula.

Australian soldiers in the jungle at Sattelberg.

destroyers off the coast, the 20 Brigade went ashore at 'Scarlet Beach', north of Finschhafen. Despite some Japanese opposition the troops forged inland quickly until stiff resistance at Katika slowed them down. The battle raged until the Japanese withdrew close to sunset. Next day the Australians were attacked by Japanese aircraft, but these were driven off by the USAAF.

Closer to Finschhafen fighting became more concentrated. The 20 Brigade struck determined defence at the Bumi River; the 2/15 Battalion skirted around. Further heavy going was encountered about Jivevaneng, inland from Katika. Allied leaders received indications that Japanese forces were massing around Sattelberg Mission, west of Jivevaneng. The Japanese also launched a severe attack on the 'Scarlet Beach' area, where supplies and further troops were still being brought ashore after the initial landings.

A soldier carries a wounded comrade back from the front lines at Sattelberg. (National Library of Australia photo)

Sergeant Derrick raises the Australian flag at Sattelberg. Derrick won the VC for his part in the action.

In the face of the Australian offensive the Japanese evacuated Finschhafen on 1 October. Advancing units of the 2/43 Battalion were attacked on the road between Jivevaneng and Sattelberg on 3 October; the ensuing battle was difficult and bloody with numerous casualties. A contingent of Australian reinforcements was rushed up from the coast to support the 2/43 Battalion. On 5 October the 2/17 Battalion took Kumawa and almost immediately was subjected to a strong counter-attack which it repelled.

For a week there was sporadic fighting as both sides tried to improve

their strategic positions. On 16 October the Japanese launched a counter-attack against Australian forces at Jivevaneng and Katika by ground and against Finschhafen by air, as well as pushing north against the 2/43 Battalion. The enemy took Katika on 19 October and held it for two weeks. Their supply lines stretched to the limit, the Japanese advance ran out of steam as quickly as it had started. The Allies pushed the Japanese back to positions around Sattelberg.

Plans were then made for an assault on Sattelberg itself. On 5 November the 20 Brigade took on the

Japanese at Jivevaneng, clearing the way for the advance on Sattelberg. Supported by tanks, the 2/48 Battalion began pushing west from Jivevaneng on 17 November while the 2/23 and 2/24 Battalions moved north from Kumawa. Three days later Australian forces engaged the enemy at Steeple Tree Hill, scoring a decisive victory. On the same day the 2/32 Battalion took Pabu Knoll. A strong force thrown around Pabu by the Japanese isolated the 2/32 Battalion for a fierce counter-attack, but the Australians held their position.

As fighting progressed it became obvious that the Japanese defence lacked co-ordination and their units were being used haphazardly. The 2/48 and 2/23 Battalions reached an area just south of Sattelberg by 22 November; two days later an attack by a company of the 2/48 Battalion forced the enemy out of the village. One of the company's number, Sergeant Derrick, was awarded the Victoria Cross for his efforts.

North of Katika the 2/28 Battalion pushed its way into enemy territory in late November to take the village of Gusika. A week later the 2/23 Battalion had moved north from Sattelberg to defeat Japanese around the Song River.

The northern advance continued through December. When the 4 Brigade had pushed through to the Masaweng River it was relieved by the 20 Brigade, thus maintaining pressure on the withdrawing enemy forces. On 13 January the 20 Brigade took the base at Nambariwa where Japanese supplies from New Britain arrived by barge.

MARKHAM AND RAMU VALLEYS

Aspectacular action began on 5 September 1943 as paratroopers in a fleet of eighty-seven Douglas C47 aircraft left Port Moresby for Nadzab in the Markham Valley. The invasion from the sky took place without opposition.

The 2/25 Battalion was involved in a major battle with entrenched Japanese forces in the Markham Valley. Heavy artillery and aerial bombardment finally dislodged the defenders, whom Allied commanders assumed were withdrawing to the north. That escape route was blocked by the 2/24 Battalion and the 2/4 Independent Company, but the Japanese evaded capture by moving westward instead.

Units of the 21 Brigade at Nadzab were detailed to engage Japanese retreating from Lae; however they proved elusive and some 8000 enemy troops escaped to other Japanese strongholds in the Ramu Valley and around Finschhafen.

While the battle raged on the Huon Peninsula, units of the 7 Division moved up the Markham River Valley towards the Ramu River. On 19 September the 2/6 Independent Company took the Japanese positions at Kaiapit, ninety kilometres west of Lae, and cleared the airstrip ready for supply aircraft. Around sunset on 21 September a company of the 2/16 Battalion was flown into Kaiapit.

Within a week the 21 Brigade had pushed forward from Kaiapit to Dumpu, allowing engineering units to begin construction of a large air base at Gusap. Such a base would allow troop reinforcements and supplies to be flown into the region easily while fighters and bombers could carry out strikes against Japanese positions.

By 5 October the 21 Brigade was

A patrol moves through swampy ground in the Finnistere Range.

moving into the mountainous areas around the Ramu River. Pushing up the Uria River, Kumbarum was wrested from Japanese control. The next advance was along the Faria River to Shaggy Ridge and Kankiryo Saddle where Japanese were firmly entrenched on the high ground. On 12 October the enemy attacked the 2/14 and 2/27 Battalions as they attempted to take Shaggy Ridge.

At Evapia River the enemy attacked the 2/25 Battalion on 13 December and forced the Australians back across the water. But the Japanese troops once again found their supply lines too long to be maintained and had to withdraw.

At Shaggy Ridge the Australians were making little headway. Then on 27 December a full-scale assault using RAAF Vengeance dive-bombers and a heavy artillery bombardment resulted in units of the 2/16 Battalion clearing the enemy from the southern end of

A wounded soldier has his cigarette lit by a native bearer at Dumpu.
(National Library of Australia photo)

the ridge. Reinforcements from the 2/10 and 2/12 Battalions moved up to Shaggy Ridge for a new offensive. On 20 January 1944 the 2/10th launched a major attack against the enemy, providing a diversion to allow the 2/12th to make a stealthy advance up the southern slopes. The Japanese, on the defensive, began pulling back, and on 26 January were driven from Kankiryo Saddle in a ferocious battle. By the end of the month the Japanese were in retreat.

February was spent consolidating hard-won gains north of the Ramu River. During March the 57/60 Battalion took the initiative and pushed north to Yokopi while the 58/59 Battalion followed the Kabenau River to the coast. On 21 March the 58/59th met up with American units which had landed in Astrolabe Bay near Bogadjim. This combined force fought its way through to the coast and the 57/60 Battalion took Bogadjim on 13 April.

An Australian soldier with a German Shepherd dog used as a messenger between units in forward battle areas around the Faria River. (National Library of Australia photo)

Troops hauling logs to construct a bridge over the Gusap River.

Climbing through the rugged Finnistere Range.

Bringing out the wounded.

North of Astrolabe Bay was the next objective: Madang. It was thought the Japanese would defend the town vigorously; however when patrols entered Madang on 24 April 1944 they found it all but deserted. The region from Lae through the Markham Valley, the Ramu Valley and down the coast to Madang was now secure.

This was the only way to scale some of the rugged mountains found in the Ramu and Markham Valleys.

BOUGAINVILLE

Troops await supplies being dropped by parachute from C47 aircraft.

As the American forces headed north to the Philippines it was decided that Australians would take over a number of key locations including the islands of Bougainville and New Britain and around Aitape on the New Guinea mainland.

First to be relieved was Bougainville. Between October and December 1944 the 7, 11, 15, 23 and 29 Brigades landed on the island. Previously the Americans and the Japanese had existed on Bougainville in a stand-off; the only action was between the Japanese- and Australian-led units of native soldiers fighting guerrilla-fashion. On 29 December the Australians broke the unofficial truce.

Australian units moved north-west to the Genga River where they engaged entrenched Japanese defenders. The 31/51 Battalion pushed through to assault enemy positions at Downs Ridge near Soraken on 19 February 1945, and late in the month was relieved by the 26 Battalion. Slowly the Japanese were driven across the Compton and Nagam Rivers until their resistance collapsed, leaving them boxed in around Buka Passage and on Buka Island.

The Japanese defended Buka Island fiercely. In an abortive assault units of the 31/51 Battalion were put ashore on 8 June at Porton Plantation under cover from land-based artillery. Japanese resistance was ferocious and the following day the men were withdrawn. Two landing-craft made it to safety, but a third struck a coral reef. Sixty men were left living on board in the half-submerged craft for two days.

Stiff opposition was encountered in the south-west around the Tavera River by the 29 Brigade as it advanced towards Buin on a number of fronts. While it was engaged at Tavera River the 47 Battalion moved to the Adele River. By the end of the month the 61 Battalion was near Kupon along the Pagana River. To aid the south-west advance a company of the 25 Battalion was landed south of Motupena Point.

During March the Japanese were being pushed further into the south-east. On 14 March their strong defence of Slater's Knoll, south of the Puriata River, against an attack by the 25 Battalion was successful. With the aid of tanks the Australians advanced against the Japanese once more and Slater's Knoll fell, but it was to be the scene of many more bloody counter-attacks before the region was secured.

On 17 April the Australians were advancing on two fronts — inland where the 57/60 Battalion operated and on the coast where the 2/24 Battalion moved along the Buin Road. The advance bogged down until the Australians took the initiative and pushed through to reach Hongorai River on 2 May, slowed by mines along the road. Over the next three days the enemy staged strong counter-attacks, including heavy artillery bombardment.

As the Japanese withdrew south to the Hari River on 17 May they were followed by the 58/59 Battalion, and on 12 June the 58/59 crossed the Hari to begin enclosing the Japanese forces. Inland the 57/60 Battalion made its way to Rusei, while the 8 Commando Squadron pushed the Japanese out of Morokaimoro on the upper reaches of the Mivo River. Engineer units began work on a landing-strip for light aircraft.

Fighting dropped to occasional skirmishes during July when torrential rains halted the advance at the swollen Mivo River. Australian units in the south-west were cut off from their supply lines. Floods subsided in early August 1945, but word was received of an imminent surrender by Japan. All patrol activities on Bougainville ceased during the second week of August.

Inside a Douglas C47 transport aircraft airmen prepare to drop supplies to troops in the jungles on Bougainville.

Matilda tanks supporting infantry in an advance on Bougainville.

NEW BRITAIN

Soldiers bringing supplies ashore at Jacquinot Bay.

On the island of New Britain was the largest Japanese force in the region, garrisoned near the town of Rabaul. Rabaul was also the headquarters of the Japanese 8 Area Army. As was the case on Bougainville, although the Americans had established bases on New Britain they had made no attempt to extend their territory beyond a wide perimeter. The Japanese had withdrawn behind a heavily defended boundary in the north-eastern corner of the Gazelle Peninsula. The Americans and Japanese were content to live and let live.

In November 1944 the 6 Brigade landed at Jacquinot Bay on the southern side of the island while the 36 Battalion was sent north to Cape Hoskins. Units went ashore against only minor resistance. Reinforcements in the form of the 13 Brigade arrived in late November.

Substantial operations began in January 1945 when the 36 Battalion, joined by the 1 New Guinea Battalion, advanced north to Ea Ea. On the opposite side of the island the 32 Battalion

Landing-craft sailing towards New Britain for the landing at Jacquinot Bay.

was engaged in similar activities, pushing north as far as Kamandran. The 19 Battalion crossed the Mevelo River on its way north to Rabaul and was met by entrenched Japanese troops around Henry Reid Bay.

Once the southern end of the Gazelle Peninsula had been cleared and the Japanese cornered there was no large-scale advance. The Australian units concentrated mainly on patrolling northward and dealing with the enemy as and when required.

A wrecked ship in Jacquinot Bay.

General Blamey and accompanying officers come ashore on New Britain to inspect Australian units.

AITAPE

On the New Guinea mainland the 6 Division was assigned to relieve American units at Aitape. All troops were landed during November 1944, but delivery of supplies dragged on until March 1945. The air base at Aitape was predominantly RAAF, with the 71 Wing flying Bristol Beaufort bombers. Lacking were transport aircraft, only one Douglas C47 being stationed there.

Short of supplies, the Australians could do little more than small-scale patrolling during November. In December the 7 Commando Squadron moved inland against considerable enemy opposition to establish a base in the Torricelli Ranges. Moving east along the coast, the 4 Battalion struck resistance at the Danmap River on 17 December. Five days later the Japanese were finally pushed back.

Replacing the 4 Battalion, the 11 Battalion took the fight to Matapau where opposition was more intense. The Australians were well supported by artillery and air bombardments. Heavy January rains turned the Danmap River into a raging flood, breaking a bridge constructed by engineering units. The 8 Battalion continued operating in the foothills while the 5 Battalion climbed into the Torricelli Ranges.

The single C47 based at Aitape was unable to cope with the advancing troops. On 10 January the 11 Battalion, supported by the 4 Armoured Battalion, took Dogreto Bay, creating a forward supply base for landing craft and alleviating the problem somewhat.

Australian soldiers inspecting one of a number of elaborate tunnels constructed by the Japanese around Rabaul.

Troops climbing down from landing ships to the craft which will take them to the shore at Aitape.

Late in January the Japanese started a bitter struggle to push the Australians back; three weeks later they withdrew. In the Torricelli Ranges the 5 Battalion forged through Salata, Numango, Malahun and Balif. On 19 February engineers began work on an airstrip at Balif while artillery units hauled mortars over the rugged mountains to use against the Japanese concentrations around Ilahop. The 6 Battalion continued to advance, taking Ilahop and Armimin. By late March the fighting had reached east as far as Aupik with the Japanese in retreat.

On the coast the 2 Battalion moved to within thirty kilometres of Wewak, the main Japanese stronghold.

Troops climbing the 'golden stairway' into the ranges behind Aitape.

Bridge engineers take time off for a swim at Aitape.

Taking But on 14 March provided a base for landing-craft, and the next day the strategically important But airfield was secured by the Australians. By early April, after a ferocious engagement at Tokuku Pass, the 2 Battalion had linked with the 3 Battalion to capture the mission station at Wonginara. While those preparations were being made the 7 Battalion finally drove the enemy out of Maprik in the Prince Alexander Ranges after ten days of bitter fighting. Maprik airstrip was upgraded to take C47 transports, allowing engineering units to bring in road-making equipment.

The way was now clear for the attack on Wewak. Leading the assault was the 4 Battalion which set off on 3 May, heading west. By 7 May the Japanese had abandoned Cape Wom to the Australians. At this point an unfortunate incident occurred which did nothing for

A church service conducted prior to the attack on Wewak.

Crossing a river on a pontoon bridge constructed by an engineering unit.

Soldiers moving out on a patrol.

Australian–American relations: ordered in to attack Wewak, Lockheed Lightning fighters of the USAAF struck Cape Wom by mistake, killing eleven Australians.

On 10 May Wewak Point was invaded by the 4 Battalion. Heavy artillery bombardments and infantry advancing with tank support secured the objective by the end of the day. The following morning an assault was launched on Japanese defensive positions around Wewak airfield. Just the town of Wewak was left.

To support the 4 Battalion, the 6 Cavalry (Commando) Regiment was put ashore just east of Wewak under cover from a heavy naval bombardment provided by the cruiser HMAS *Hobart* and the destroyers HMAS *Arunta* and *Warramunga* and HMS *Newfound-*

land. Working west, the Cavalrymen engaged the besieged Japanese forces until the two Australian forces linked up in Wewak on 22 May. The last battle of the war in New Guinea took place on 8 August 1945 when the 2 New Guinea Battalion and 7 Battalion pushed out the Japanese defenders and took Kiarivu.

During these last three months of the war air support by the RAAF was hampered by an acute shortage of bombs and the air force was reduced to using captured enemy bombs. This did nothing to allay the feeling of the troops in New Guinea as the end of the war approached that they were the forgotten army.

On guard at the beach near Aitape.

An American landing ship caught in the mud at the Tarakan landings.

LAST DAYS

The war effort moved out of Australian territory in May 1945 when Allied commanders decided to mount an attack on Borneo. Japanese forces in the South-West Pacific region were being increasingly isolated as the Americans advanced north. In Australia questions were asked about the wisdom of more large-scale landings and battles when the Japanese were close to defeat. There seemed little sense in losing more lives in attacks that might have no value to the conduct of the war.

Despite these doubts it was decided to proceed with three landings by Australian forces in Borneo. The first would take place at Tarakan Island, the second in the Brunei Bay – Labuan Island area and the last at Balikpapan.

Australians engaged in a battle for an airstrip in the Tarakan operation.

An Australian soldier with a liberated Indonesian.

TARAKAN

In late April 1945 an invasion fleet escorted by the cruiser HMAS *Hobart* and the destroyers HMAS *Barcoo, Burdekin, Hawkesbury, Lachlan* and *Warramunga* arrived off the south-western coast of Tarakan. Supported by heavy naval bombardment, on 30 April engineers destroyed the tangle of defences blocking a landing at Tarakan Island.

Preceded by another naval bombardment and with heavy air cover, the 23 and 48 Battalions went ashore against only light opposition the following day. Quickly moving inland, the first real obstruction to the troops was at Lingkas Hill where entrenched Japanese units engaged the Australians. While the 23 Battalion continued its swift advance the 48th engaged the Japanese at the high point, code-named 'Lyons'. The airfield fell after a fierce battle. Then, on 3 May, the 4 Commando Squadron attacked Tarakan Hill, suffering many casualties but overcoming the Hill by sunset. Next day the Japanese were driven from the Tarakan township, but for nine days heavy fighting continued against a dogged Japanese defence.

Flame-throwers were used to dislodge Japanese forces from underground bunkers and pill-boxes.

LABUAN

Brunei Bay on the north-western coast of Borneo was the site for the next Australian offensive. The assault took place on 10 June 1945 on two fronts — one on the island of Labuan, the other on the mainland and a small island at the western edge of the Bay near Brooketon.

On 9 May the 3 Pioneer Battalion bailed up the enemy on a hill code-named 'Helen'. All efforts to shift them proved fruitless: in spite of a savage naval bombardment followed by concentrated air strikes the Japanese were immovable. This impasse was broken on 14 May when USAAF aircraft dropped napalm, finally driving the Japanese from their bunkers.

At the Japanese headquarters at Fukukaku the defenders stood their ground, prepared for a fight to the death. The Australians were now employing flame-throwers to displace the stubborn Japanese. From 18 to 25 May all assaults ended in failure until a combination of aerial bombing, mortar bombardment, napalm and an infantry assault triumphed.

Sporadic resistance on Tarakan Island continued through May and into June 1945. But the Japanese forces were short of supplies and their numbers had been severely depleted.

A landing ship en route to Labuan.

Jeeps moving ashore at Labuan. (National Library of Australia)

On Labuan Island two Battalions, the 28th and the 43rd, went ashore just east of Labuan township. Finding no opposition from the Japanese they moved inland until they encountered some resistance, particularly around Flagstaff Hill. By nightfall the airfield was theirs. Once the Australians had control of most of Labuan Island and Japanese resistance was concentrated in an area called 'The Pocket' north of the township, as on Tarakan the Japanese seemed prepared to die defending what they had left. Heavy bombardment from ships off shore failed to break their determination and they even staged an unsuccessful counter-attack on Labuan town. Resistance at 'The Pocket' was ultimately broken by the infantry wielding flame-throwers.

The 15 Battalion had landed on Muara Island to find it completely unoccupied, while the 17 Battalion had gone ashore on the mainland at Brunei Bluff. Against little opposition the 17th pushed south-west as far as Brunei township, taking it on 13 June and gaining control of the airfield. They advanced around Brunei Bay to take Lingkungan and within days the Klias Peninsula region was secure.

In pursuit of Japanese troops, the 17 Battalion entered Seria on 21 June to find the enemy had set fire to most of the town's oil wells. Black smoke choked the sky for days before engineering units could stop the blazes. Meanwhile the 32 Battalion moved north-east along the railway line to Papar. On 26 June the 32 and 43 Battalions approached Beaufort along the Padas River. After a heavy

fight over two days they won the town. Late on the 28th the Japanese counter-attacked then withdrew into well-fortified positions around Beaufort.

Upon landing at Lutong the 13 Battalion discovered numerous emaciated, diseased, Indian prisoners of war. The Australians learned of the horrific treatment of Indian soldiers at the hands of the Japanese and of wholesale slaughter of the men who had defended Borneo in 1941 and '42.

By late June the remnants of the Japanese forces had been pushed inland. The Australians elected not to follow. Now the military was involved in something new: civil administration. The British Borneo Civil Affairs Unit, staffed by Australian and British officers, arrived to organise relief for the population and commence the rebuilding of devastated towns and villages.

Indian soldiers freed from a Japanese POW camp at Lutong.

Troops inspecting a badly damaged oil refinery at Lutong.

An Australian patrol moves past a dead Japanese on Labuan.

Equipment being loaded aboard landing ships for the assault on Balikpapan.

BALIKPAPAN

To Australians, the last major action of the Pacific War was also the most controversial. Considerable argument raged as to whether the attack on Balikpapan on the south-eastern coast of Borneo, which began on 1 July 1945, was a gross waste of Australian manpower. At that stage the war had six weeks left to run.

The assault went ahead. For two weeks before the invasion Allied minesweepers cleared huge numbers of mines placed in Balikpapan harbour by both sides. A convoy of 100 ships landed the 18 and 21 Brigades south of Balikpapan township.

First ashore at Klandasan, just south of Balikpapan, were the 16 and 27 Battalions. Their advances differed considerably: the latter found the going easy while the former pushed forward in the face of considerable opposition. The day after the Australians took command of Mount Malang the Sepinggang airfield fell to the 14 Battalion without opposition. Tough opposition from Japanese entrenched in the hills was encountered by the 25 Brigade.

On 4 July, although hampered by Japanese in the surrounding hills, Australian troops captured the Manggar airfield. Several heavy naval guns possessed by the enemy did considerable damage to Australian tanks, so that night Australian patrols attacked and took the gun positions. In the north the 25 Brigade was advancing along the Milford Highway against violent resistance. Australian units suffered considerable losses between 4 July and 9 July.

By 21 July the enemy had withdrawn through the village of Batuchampar, fighting doggedly all the way. When the enemy pulled back into the hills the Australians opted not to follow.

Troops travelling ashore from transport ships in 'alligators', American amphibious landing-craft.

The other front in the Balikpapan operation opened on the western side of Balikpapan Bay on 5 July. Its aim was to neutralise any Japanese action which might threaten ships crowded into the Bay. Real resistance was not encountered until 7 July, and even that was half-hearted. The 9 Battalion advanced easily against only sporadic battles with the enemy.

Australian soldiers going ashore on American landing-craft at Balikpapan.

Gunners in action at Balikpapan.

The news of Japan's surrender reaches troops at Balikpapan.

Liberated prisoners of war at the gates of the infamous Changi prison camp.

THE END

By 15 August 1945 it was all over. Although many Australians saw the Balikpapan operation as a futile effort in which a number of Australians died for no real gain, their misgivings were swamped in the waves of euphoria which swept the world.

Former Australian prisoners of war liberated from Changi in 1945.

General Blamey signs the Japanese surrender document on behalf of Australia at Yokohama Bay.

The first Australian troops to arrive in Japan after the surrender.

Japanese soldiers are questioned by Australian officers.   89

Delousing clothes of liberated POWs in Japan.

Liberated Australian POWs at Kuching.

Captured Japanese at Kuching.

Surrendered Japanese soldiers.

Japanese POWs on the island of Morotai.

Captured Japanese troops building an airstrip at Koepang, Timor.

Home at last.

Crowds in Martin Place, Sydney, celebrate the announcement of the Japanese surrender.

Hundreds of thousands of people gathered in Sydney's Hyde Park for a thanksgiving service shortly after the Japanese surrender.

A former POW welcomed home by his family.